INTRODUCTION

Chocolate is one of the products that is all too often overlooked in a wholefooder's diet. On the premise that 'a little bit of what you fancy does you good', chocolate is consumed as a treat, a small 'won't-do-me-any-harm' indulgence, a nightly reward for keeping to a calorie-controlled diet, a soother and comforter.

For some, chocolate holds the same addictive properties that alcohol has for alcoholics – a passion that is indulged in often with the utmost secrecy. For others it is psychological pick-me-up eaten during depression and emotionally disturbed moments, often as a substitute for love and affection.

In spite of the fact that many of us consider eating chocolate a 'sin', we nevertheless continue to consume it, as a nation, in large quantities, regardless of its alleged association with migraine, obesity, acne, tooth decay, diabetes and coronary diseases. So great is our love affair with chocolate that we conveniently choose to forget about the harmful reactions that it can produce in our bodies.

Chocolate's Methylxanthine Content

Most people are aware that chocolate is produced from the cocoa bean, but what is not generally known is that both chocolate and cocoa contain caffeine and theobromine, both chemical substances that are classed as methylxanthines. Theophylline, which is present in tea, is also classed as a methylxanthine.

Methylxanthines stimulate both the central nervous system and the cardiovascular system, increase the amount of gastric acid that is secreted in the stomach and have a diuretic effect on the kidneys. To put it more plainly, the caffeine and theobromine contained in chocolate and cocoa can play havoc with your nerves, make your heart beat faster and give you an upset tummy.

Research that has recently been carried out indicates that mothers who breast-feed their babies should eliminate chocolate from their diet during the nursing period. This is because caffeine and theobromine are passed onto the baby through the mother's milk, producing a certain amount of hyperactivity and other undesirable reactions in the baby, such as irritability and a proneness to diarrhoea, eczema and constipation.

A link has also been discovered between fibrocystic breast disease – a condition characterized by fibrous tissue and cyst fluid in the breast – and consumption of methylxanthines such as those found in chocolate, cocoa, coffee, tea and cola drinks. Dr John Minton's extensive research on this female disorder led him to discover that 47 women who were suffering from this disease all consumed, on average, 190mg of methylxanthines each day. Most of the women who eliminated all sources of methylxanthines from their diet found that the condition disappeared completely

THE CAROB COOKBOOK

A fascinating collection of recipes making use of carob powder (made from dried locust beans), the alternative to caffeine-containing chocolate.

THE CAROB COOKBOOK

by

LORRAINE WHITESIDE

THORSONS PUBLISHERS LIMITED
Wellingborough, Northamptonshire

First published 1981

British Library Cataloguing in Publication Data

Whiteside, Lorraine
　The carob cookbook
　1. Carob
　2. Cookery
　I. Title
　641.6446　　TX813.C/

ISBN 0-7225-0726-7

Photoset by Ad' House, Earls Barton, Northamptonshire.
Printed and bound in Great Britain by
Richard Clay (The Chaucer Press), Bungay, Suffolk.

CONTENTS

PREFACE

Interest in natural food is increasing along with a growing awareness and acceptance of the importance of good nutrition in ensuring a healthy body and mind for life. Whilst a young person may have boundless vitality and energy on a junk food diet, in twenty years time that same person may well turn out to be a very unfit middle-aged individual.

Basing our diet on natural, unrefined foods is in all probability one of the most sensible and effective measures against ill health that we may ever take. As youngsters we give little thought to health and nutrition – our carefree lives are spent expending that seemingly infinite energy that we are naturally born with. But as the years pass we begin to realize that taking care of ourselves, becoming aware of how our bodies work and taking an interest in the foods we eat, is rewarding and above all necessary if we are to enjoy a long and illness-free existence.

Unfortunately, the majority of us spend some part of our lives abusing our bodies by eating and drinking too much of the wrong kind of things. Many people, albeit unknowingly, abuse their bodies throughout their entire lifetime.

The outstanding development of food technology that has taken place in this century has given us packaged convenience foods, a whole array of tinned foods with their chemical preservatives and even so-called 'fun foods' that are marketed and commercialized with little regard for the long-term effects on our health. The awful legacy of all this is that a lifetime of poor nutrition is endured by many of us with the inevitable increased susceptibility to troublesome illnesses and degenerative diseases.

Thankfully, most caring and health-orientated people now realize that many foods that have in the past been labelled 'pure', such as white sugar and white flour, are empty foods with little or no nutritive value. The trend is now towards turning back to Mother Nature, eating the natural foods of the earth and renouncing the refining and preservation processes that are the product of a so-called civilized society. Ironically, in the case of food products, civilization has bred destruction.

Carob is one of the many health foods that is enjoying increasing popularity. Although it has been eaten by man for centuries, it has only recently been used as an alternative to chocolate. Unfortunately, the disadvantages of chocolate and cocoa consumption are little publicized and I am sure that many parents are unaware of the possible harm that an excessive intake of chocolate may be doing to their children, or the effect that it may be having on their behaviour. Fortunately, a healthy alternative to chocolate can now be offered to children and adults alike, one which I am sure will go on rising in popularity as junk foods fall from favour and natural wholefoods take their rightful place in human nutrition.

within two months to one year.

Chocolate's Allergenic Properties

Chocolate is one of the most common allergens, capable of triggering off headaches, migraine, depression, mental confusion, anxiety, panic attacks, hyperactivity, even hallucinations and violent behaviour. Some other common allergens are eggs, wheat, cow's milk, sugar, coffee, to name but a few.

In his book *Not all in the Mind* (Pan, 1976), the leading British allergy expert, Dr Richard Mackarness, puts forward his belief that food and chemical allergies may be responsible for disorders of the respiratory system, the skin, the digestive system, the cardiovascular system, the musculo-skeletal system, the central nervous system, the genito-urinary system, the mind and the endocrine system. Dr Mackarness also says that 30 per cent of people seeking medical attention show symptoms that are directly related to a food or chemical allergy.

Dr Arthur Coca, who pioneered allergy research in the United States, is convinced that 90 per cent of the population is likely to suffer from food allergies. A survey carried out by Dr Coca amongst 100 patients demonstrated that 17 out of the group were allergic to chocolate. The most common allergy was to eggs, with 33 of the patients showing allergic reactions.

One of the major causes for concern is that a lot of allergies go undetected. Many individuals are inclined to relate the unpleasant symptoms to other disorders, not suspecting that they may be suffering from an intolerance to one or several types of food. Fatigue, irritability, palpitations or other unusual symptoms are indicative of a possible food allergy.

If you would like to find out if you are allergic to

chocolate or any other foodstuffs, try the pulse test put forward by Dr Coca in his book *The Pulse Test – Easy Allergy Detection**. As the pulse rate is believed to speed up after consuming a food allergen, Dr Coca suggests that the pulse be taken on waking and at periodic intervals during the day, particularly after eating. In Dr Coca's estimation, a pulse rate of more than 84 beats per minute could be produced by an allergic reaction.

If you notice any unpleasant symptoms after eating chocolate or drinking cocoa and have a noticeably increased pulse rate, the chances are that you are allergic to them.

Chocolate's Oxalic Acid Content

Although there is calcium in the cocoa bean, a significant amount of oxalic acid is also present, which renders the calcium unavailable to the body. When calcium combines with oxalic acid during digestion, it forms calcium oxalate, an insoluble compound that is incapable of being absorbed by the body. Thus calcium that is consumed in conjunction with oxalic acid passes through the system without being assimilated. Because of this, when cocoa or drinking chocolate is added to milk, the nutritive value of the calcium normally obtained when the milk is drunk alone, is destroyed.

Carob, the Healthy Alternative

Delectable though chocolate may be, its nutritional disadvantages combined with the potentially harmful allergic reactions and stimulating effects that it produces have given rise to the need for a harmless,

* Distributed in the U.K. by Thorsons.

yet equally delicious alternative. Carob has been found to be that alternative.

Carob has enjoyed recognition in health food circles in the United States for some years and its popularity in the United Kingdom is increasing along with the growing demand for natural foods and the awareness that a healthy diet is reflected in a healthy body and mind. In the same way that honey and molasses are being used in place of refined sugar, wholemeal flour instead of white and fresh, additive-free foods instead of tinned and processed items, now chocolate, which has impassioned so many of us for so long, has a substitute.

The Carob Tree and Its Origin

The carob tree (Ceratonia siliqua) originated in the Middle East and later spread to countries bordering the Mediterranean Sea such as Italy, Spain, Morocco, Greece and Cyprus. The tree flourishes in these warm climates and in many areas it grows uncultivated. The carob tree was introduced into the United States about a century ago and is grown in southern regions where the climate is similar to that of the Mediterranean countries.

The carob tree is a large evergreen which bears glossy brown edible seed pods which grow to about 4-12 inches in length and 1-2 inches in width, and contain a sweet-tasting edible pulp. Although the tree takes about 50 years to reach its fully-grown height of 40-50 feet and only begins to yield fruit on a regular basis after 15 years, it lives to a very great age and will go on producing fruit for many years.

The fruit is also known as the 'locust bean', or 'St John's Bread' as the pods were said to have provided nourishment for St John the Baptist in the wilderness.

It is also said that the husks or pods were the food on which the prodigal son survived.

The carob fruit has for centuries been considered a valuable source of nourishment for man and beast, and the hard seeds that nestle within the pods were once used by goldsmiths and jewellers as a standard for measuring the weight of gold and precious stones. Indeed, the word 'carat', still in use today, is derived from the name given to the seeds of the carob fruit.

How Carob Powder is Made

Carob powder is made from carefully selected pods of the carob tree which are washed to remove any foreign bodies. The pulp is then separated from the pod by means of a coarse-grinding process, after which the pulp is sieved, roasted and blended into a fine powder which is similar in flavour and texture to cocoa powder.

Carob's Nutritional Advantages

The nutritional advantages of carob must inevitably be compared with the disadvantages of chocolate, although far from being just a substitute, carob is a nutritive food in its own right. Carob powder's 8 per cent protein content is relatively high when compared with other vegetable products. It is also a good source of vitamins A, D, B_1 (thiamin), B_2 (riboflavin) and B_3 (niacin). Carob, in fact, provides as much thiamin as asparagus or strawberries, its riboflavin content is equivalent to that of brown rice and it contains as much niacin as lima beans or dates. Good quantities of several important minerals are also present, including calcium, magnesium and potassium, as well as the trace minerals iron, manganese, barium, chromium, copper and nickel. It is little wonder with its high nutritive value that the carob tree is also known as the 'Tree of life'.

When carob is compared with chocolate, its advantages become very clear. To begin with, carob contains no caffeine or theobromine, the harmful substances which, as mentioned, may produce several undesirable reactions in our systems. It has none of the allergenic properties associated with chocolate and cocoa. Nor does it contain any oxalic acid, the substance that renders calcium unavailable to the body. Furthermore, carob powder contains less fat and less sodium than cocoa powder and has a higher crude fibre content. As it is made up of approximately 46 per cent natural sugars, including fructose, carob requires less sweetening than chocolate or cocoa powder.

Medicinal Value of Carob's Pectin Content

Carob's principal medicinal value lies in its high pectin content, a gelatinous water-soluble substance which occurs naturally in fruits on ripening and which is used as a gelling agent in jams and jellies. Pectin is particularly valuable for regulating the digestion and protecting the body naturally against diarrhoea.

Carob powder has been used successfully in the United States, Canada and Europe in the prevention and treatment of diarrhoea in children, when the condition is caused specifically by a digestive upset, heat or fatigue rather than by a germ or as a result of a more serious complaint. Digestive disorders such as this are fairly recurrent in young children and are particularly distressing for the parents. Experiments with carob powder have produced good results when given to children at a 5 per cent concentration, that is

Comparison of Carob Powder with Cocoa Powder
(based on a typical analysis)

	Carob Powder	Cocoa Powder
Calories per 100g	177	295
Crude Fat	0.7%	23.7%
Carbohydrates:		
Natural Sugars	46.0%	5.5%
Crude Fibre	7.0%	4.3%
Other Carbohydrates		
(by difference)	35.4%	38.5%
Crude Protein	4.5%	16.8%
Ash	3.4%	8.2%
Moisture	3.0%	3.0%
Iron (mg/100g)	50	10
Sodium (mg/100g)	100	700
Potassium (mg/100g)	950	650
Caffeine	Nil	0.16%
Theobromine	Nil	1.1%

The above table kindly supplied by Granary Foods Ltd.
of Burton-on-Trent.

one tablespoonful to 8 fl oz (225ml) of warm milk. In most cases the disorder cleared up within approximately 24 hours. Reports of such experiments have been published in the Journal of the Canadian Medical Association and the U.S. *Journal of Pediatrics.*

Carob also contains lignin, which like pectin, is recognized as a digestion regulator and for its protective properties against diarrhoea, particularly in children.

Other Medicinal Values

The Carob fruit is also highly valued in the Middle East and Asia for its medicinal properties. In the Middle East a decoction of the fruit is made and the water in which it has been boiled is drunk to relieve catarrhal infections. In Asia, particularly India, the pods are known for their astringent properties and are used to counteract coughs.

Is Carob Fattening?

Like all sweet things, carob can be fattening when taken in excess but compared with chocolate or cocoa it has a much lower calorie content. One hundred grams of cocoa powder will add 295 calories to your diet whereas the same amount of carob powder rates only 177 calories. So, for those of us who need to watch our weight yet find it difficult to resist the temptation of a little bit of sweetness, carob will do less damage to the waistline than chocolate. With its lower calorie content, carob can be more easily incorporated into a 1,000 calorie a day diet, and you can rest in the knowledge that your 'once-a-day-treat' is far more than just junk food.

How to Use Carob

Carob powder can be used in any recipe as a substitute for cocoa powder. Its distinctive chocolate-like flavour combines well with fresh and dried fruits, nuts, honey and yogurt, and it can be used in endless ways to make delicious, nutritious cakes, biscuits and desserts.

Carob is also available in block form, just like a bar of chocolate and is without doubt a firm favourite with the children. It can be melted over hot water to be added to your recipes or to make a delicious sauce.

Also, it can be bought in the form of an instant beverage which can be made into a night-cap just by adding hot milk or water.

A Word About the Other Ingredients

Wholemeal Flour

If the health of your family is your main concern, you should not consider using anything but 100 per cent wholemeal flour for all your baking. It is a vital part of healthy eating, providing an excellent source of fibre, and is the richest known source of vitamin E. It also contains a significant amount of the B vitamins and protein.

Wholemeal flour is of course much coarser in texture than white flour, and you may at first find it more difficult to handle. But you can be certain that your family will applaud the improved flavour of cakes, teabreads, biscuits, puddings and pastries made with wholemeal flour.

Polyunsaturated Margarine

The fat ingredient used in all the recipes is poly-unsaturated margarine. This is by personal choice and you may of course prefer to use butter. However, there has been much research into the causes of atherosclerosis (a condition resulting from fatty substances being deposited on the arterial walls) and it is evident that one of the major causes is the intake of a high proportion of saturated fats. These fatty deposits may produce partial blockages, thickening the arterial wall and thus narrowing the size of the channel through which the blood passes. In advanced cases strokes or coronary occlusions may result.

Saturated fats can be recognized by their solidity at

room temperature – butter, lard and meat fat for example. Unsaturated fats on the other hand are liquid fats derived from vegetables and cereals. Oils which are highest in polyunsaturates are safflower, sunflower, soya, corn and wheat germ. One of the principal values of vegetable oils is their high linoleic acid content which is needed by the body before particles of fat can be broken down and utilized.

Both the United Kingdom Medical Research Council and the United States Senate Select Committee have advised the public to reduce their saturated fat intake and there would seem to be little doubt that increased usage of unsaturated fats is a sensible measure to take in the prevention of ill-health.

The most popular polyunsaturated margarines are those made from sunflower and corn oils. These are ideal for baking, particularly if your aim is to reduce the proportion of saturated fats consumed by your family.

Raw Cane Sugar
In many countries, the purer and whiter the sugar, the better it is believed to be, but no belief could be more erroneous. The sugar refining process removes all the valuable vitamins and minerals, leaving an end-product that is pure carbohydrate and totally devoid of nutrients.

The residue that remains when the sugar refining process is completed is known as molasses and until recently it was only thought to be fit for animal consumption, but it has at last been justly recognized as a valuable source of vitamins and minerals in human nutrition. Molasses is a particularly good source of the B vitamins and is rich in iron, copper, calcium, phosphorus and potassium.

Raw cane sugar contains varying degrees of molasses and, generally speaking, the darker the sugar, the greater its nutritional value, as the colour of the sugar indicates the amount of molasses it contains. A very dark, almost black sugar therefore has a higher proportion of molasses than a lighter coloured sugar.

However, not all brown sugar is natural raw cane sugar. Certain types of so-called 'brown' sugar are simply white sugar that has been coloured. The way to check whether brown sugar is genuine raw cane sugar or not is to put a spoonful into a glass of water and if it turns white as it sinks to the bottom, it is not. To be absolutely sure that you are buying genuine raw cane sugar, always choose brands which state the country of origin on the packet and wherever possible buy your sugar from health food stores where you will find genuine Muscovado and Barbados sugars.

Honey

Renowned for its curative and healing properties, honey has been used by man throughout the ages. The prophet Mohammed said: 'Honey is a remedy for all ills', and Solomon's advice was: 'My son, eat thou honey for it is good'. The ancient Egyptians applied honey to burns and wounds and used it as a sacrificial offering to their gods.

Honey is in fact one of the most pure sources of natural sugars. It is particularly valuable as a source of energy because the principal sugars that it contains – levulose (fructose) and dextrose (glucose) – are rapidly assimilated by the body and thus quickly converted into energy.

Honey contains vitamins A, B_1, B_2, B_3, pantothenic

acid, B$_6$, biotin, folic acid and vitamin C, and there are traces of iron, copper, sodium, potassium, calcium, magnesium, phosphorus and manganese. Honey also contains a substance known as acetylcholine which helps to increase the flow of blood to the heart whilst decreasing the blood pressure and the heart rate at the same time.

As a substitute for sugar, honey is second to none. It gives extra flavour and goodness to cakes, biscuits, puddings, hot and cold drinks – in fact any recipes in which sugar is required. You will also find that cakes stay fresh longer when honey is added owing to the increased moisture, but biscuits may lose their crispness, so unless you plan to eat them on the day that they are made, it is probably wiser to stick to raw cane sugar so that they don't become soft during storage.

Yogurt

According to an ancient Persian tradition, an angel revealed the secret of making yogurt to the prophet Abraham and to this he owed his long life and fertility. We are told in the Bible that he reached the age of 175 and became the father of a child when he was 100 years old.

Yogurt is as valued a food today as it was in ancient times. It is rich in protein, calcium and the B vitamins, and it contains health-giving bacteria known as *Lactobacillus bulgaricus* which promote the growth of other beneficial bacteria in the intestinal tract. Sufferers from digestive complaints often find yogurt helps them through its stabilizing influence on the normal lactic flora in the intestine. As it does not have the same allergenic properties that milk has, people who suffer from milk intolerance are able to take yogurt without any trouble.

Yogurt has a very significant role in a healthy eating programme and as it combines well with most foods, it can be incorporated into almost any recipe. Added to cakes, puddings, and biscuits, yogurt provides extra protein and vitamins, improved flavour and increased moisture. It can be used in place of cream and as a protein alternative to eggs.

Always choose natural, unsweetened yogurt as many of the flavoured yogurts contain preservatives, colouring and refined sugar.

RECIPES

1. CAKES AND BISCUITS

The British, as well as being a nation of tea drinkers, are also a nation of cake and biscuit eaters. There is no doubt that tea and cake make one of the most perfect combinations. But what about the nutritive value of our cakes and biscuits? Certainly the majority of shop-bought varieties fall into the 'junk food' category – prepared with refined flour, refined sugar, saturated fat and in some cases preservatives and colourings, they are of dubious nutritional value.

Home made cakes prepared with 100 per cent wholemeal flour, polyunsaturated margarine, raw cane sugar and other natural ingredients such as honey and yogurt can, on the other hand, play a significant part in a healthy diet. Although cakes and biscuits should not by any means form the major part of our diet, those made with natural ingredients are a good source of unrefined carbohydrate providing the body with energy and plenty of necessary vitamins and minerals.

The addition of carob to your wholemeal cakes and biscuits will supply extra nutrients as well as a delicious flavour that is particularly appealing to children, the majority of whom have an almost insatiable sweet tooth.

Carob Cherry Cake
(Makes 8 inch cake)

8 oz (225g) wholemeal flour
2 oz (50g) carob powder
3 level teaspoonsful baking powder
4 oz (100g) polyunsaturated margarine
6 oz (175g) glacé cherries, cut into quarters
2 tablespoonsful clear honey
2 eggs, beaten
3 tablespoonsful natural unsweetened yogurt
little milk to mix

Place the flour, carob powder and baking powder in a large mixing bowl. Rub in the margarine until the mixture resembles fine breadcrumbs. Add the *glacé* cherries.

Make a well in the centre and fold in the beaten eggs, honey and yogurt. Mix all the ingredients together thoroughly and if necessary add a little milk to give a soft dropping consistency.

Spoon the mixture into a greased and lined 8 inch round deep cake tin and bake for about 1-1½ hours at 350°F/180°C (Gas Mark 4) until the cake is well-risen and firm to the touch.

Carob Walnut and Raisin Teabread
(Makes 8 inch loaf)

6 oz (175g) polyunsaturated margarine
4 oz (100g) raw cane sugar
3 eggs, beaten
3 oz (75g) chopped walnuts
3 oz (75g) small seedless raisins

6 oz (175g) wholemeal flour
2 oz (50g) carob powder
2½ level teaspoonsful baking powder
whole walnuts (for decoration)

Cream the margarine and sugar together until light
and fluffy. Add the beaten eggs a little at a time. Fold
in the flour, baking powder and carob powder.
Finally stir in the chopped walnuts and raisins.

Put the mixture into a greased and lined 8 inch loaf
tin. Smooth over the top of the mixture and decorate
with whole walnuts. Bake for 1-1½ hours at 350°F/
180°C (Gas Mark 4).

Carob Orange Cake
(Makes one 7 inch sandwich cake)

6 oz (175g) polyunsaturated margarine
4 oz (100g) raw cane sugar
3 eggs, beaten
6 oz (175g) wholemeal flour
1 oz (25g) carob powder
2 level teaspoonsful baking powder
grated rind and juice of one orange
raw cane sugar orange curd (for filling)

Grease and line two 7 inch cake tins.

Cream the margarine and sugar together well.
Gradually add the beaten eggs and then stir in the
orange juice and rind. Fold in the flour, carob powder
and baking powder.

Divide the mixture between the two cake tins and
bake for about 25-30 minutes at 375°F/190°C (Gas Mark 5).

When cool, sandwich the cakes together with raw
cane sugar orange curd.

Carob and Apricot Teabread
(Makes 8 inch loaf)

6 oz (175g) wholemeal flour
2 oz (50g) carob powder
2 level teaspoonsful baking powder
4 oz (100g) polyunsaturated margarine
4 oz (100g) chopped dried apricots
2 oz (50g) chopped blanched almonds
2 tablespoonsful clear honey
3 tablespoonsful natural unsweetened yogurt
little milk to mix
whole blanched almonds (for decoration)

Put the flour, carob powder and baking powder into a large mixing bowl. Rub in the margarine until the mixture resembles fine breadcrumbs. Add the apricots and almonds.

Make a well in the centre and stir in the honey, yogurt and enough milk to give a dropping consistency. Mix all the ingredients together thoroughly.

Pour the mixture into an 8 inch greased and lined loaf tin, spread evenly and decorate with whole blanched almonds. Bake for about 1 hour at 350°F/ 180°C (Gas Mark 4).

Carob Banana Bread

(Makes 8 inch loaf)

6 oz (175g) wholemeal flour
2 oz (50g) carob powder
2 level teaspoonsful baking powder
4 oz (100g) polyunsaturated margarine
2 oz (50g) chopped walnuts
3 tablespoonsful clear honey
2 eggs
3 tablespoonsful natural unsweetened yogurt
1 lb (450g) ripe bananas

Peel and mash the bananas and set aside in a bowl. Put the flour, carob powder and baking powder into a large mixing bowl. Rub the margarine into the dry ingredients so that the mixture resembles fine bread-crumbs. Add the chopped walnuts.

Make a hollow in the centre and fill in with the honey, eggs, yogurt and mashed banana. Mix all the ingredients really well until a soft, runny consistency is obtained. Pour into a greased and lined 8 inch loaf tin and bake in a moderate oven at 350°F/180°C (Gas Mark 4) for about 1½ hours.

Carob and Date Teabread
(Makes 8 inch loaf)

6 oz (175g) wholemeal flour
2 oz (50g) carob powder
2 level teaspoonsful baking powder
3 oz (75g) polyunsaturated margarine
6 oz (175g) stoned dates
1 egg, beaten
2 tablespoonsful clear honey
3 tablespoonsful natural unsweetened yogurt
little milk to mix

Put the flour, carob powder and baking powder into a large mixing bowl. Rub in the margarine until the mixture resembles fine breadcrumbs.

Chop the dates and stir into the dry ingredients. Add the beaten egg, honey and yogurt, mixing thoroughly. If necessary, add a little milk to produce a dropping consistency.

Place the mixture into a greased and lined 8 inch loaf tin and bake for about 1 hour at 350°F/180°C (Gas Mark 4) until firm to the touch.

Carob Apple Cake
(Makes 8 inch cake)

4 oz (100g) polyunsaturated margarine
4 oz (100g) raw cane sugar
2 eggs, beaten
2 oz (50g) chopped hazelnuts
4 oz (100g) wholemeal flour
1½ level teaspoonsful baking powder

Filling
1 lb (450g) dessert apples
grated rind and juice of ½ lemon
2 tablespoonsful raw cane sugar

Topping
2 oz (50g) block carob
little milk to mix

Peel, core and slice the apples, and put into a saucepan with the sugar, lemon juice and rind. Cook for about 20 minutes until soft and leave to cool.

Cream the margarine and sugar together until light and fluffy. Gradually add the beaten eggs, then fold in the flour, baking powder and chopped hazelnuts.

Pour the mixture into a greased and lined 8 inch cake tin and bake for about 25-30 minutes at 350°F/ 180°C (Gas Mark 4).

When cool, split the cake in half and fill with the apple mixture. For the topping, melt the carob in a bowl over hot water, adding a little milk to soften. Spread the melted carob over the top of the cake with a palette knife.

Carob Rum Cake
(Makes 9 inch cake)

6 oz (175g) polyunsaturated margarine
2 oz (50g) raw cane sugar
2 tablespoonsful clear honey
2 eggs, beaten
6 oz (175g) wholemeal flour
2 level teaspoonsful baking powder
2 oz (50g) carob powder
2 tablespoonsful dark rum
2 tablespoonsful natural unsweetened yogurt
little milk to mix

For decoration
2 oz (50g) block carob
1 tablespoonful milk
2 oz (50g) chopped blanched almonds

Cream the margarine, sugar and honey together until light and fluffy. Gradually add the beaten eggs a little at a time. Carefully fold in the flour, baking powder and carob powder, then stir in the rum and yogurt. If necessary add a little milk to produce a dropping consistency.

Spoon the mixture into a greased and lined 9 inch cake tin and bake at 350°F/180°C (Gas Mark 4) for about 30 minutes until the cake is firm to the touch.

Whilst the cake is cooling, melt the block carob in a bowl over hot water and stir in the milk to make a smooth coating. Spoon the coating over the cake with a palette knife, allowing some of the coating to fall down the sides of the cake. Sprinkle liberally with chopped blanched almonds.

Carob and Almond Layer Cake

(Makes three layer 8 inch cake)

4 eggs
3 oz (75g) raw cane sugar
6 oz (175g) wholemeal flour
2 oz (50g) carob powder
2 level teaspoonsful baking powder

For decoration
clear honey
6 oz (175g) toasted flaked almonds

Place the eggs and sugar in a large mixing bowl and stand in a sink filled with hot water. Whisk the eggs and sugar together until thick and creamy. The whisk should leave a trail when you take it out of the mixture. Remove the basin from the hot water and fold in the flour, carob powder and baking powder.

Pour the mixture into a greased and lined rectangular baking tin (12 x 8 inches), spreading evenly. Bake at 375°F/190°C (Gas Mark 5) for about 20 minutes.

When the cake is cool, split into three equal rectangles. Spread honey on two of the rectangles and sprinkle with some of the flaked almonds. Sandwich the three layers together and spread honey over the top of the cake. Sprinkle with the remaining flaked almonds.

Carob Orange Buns
(Makes approximately 1 dozen)

2 oz (50g) polyunsaturated margarine
2 oz (50g) raw cane sugar
1 egg, beaten
3 oz (75g) wholemeal flour
1 ½ level teaspoonsful baking powder
2 oz (50g) carob powder
grated rind and juice of 1 orange
1 tablespoonful natural unsweetened yogurt

Cream the margarine and sugar together until light and fluffy. Gradually add the beaten egg. Fold in the flour, baking powder and carob powder. Stir in the orange rind, yogurt and enough of the orange juice to produce a dropping consistency.

Spoon the mixture into small paper cases and bake for about 10-15 minutes at 375°F/190°C (Gas Mark 5).

Carob Raisin Squares
(Makes approximately 10)

4 oz (100g) polyunsaturated margarine
3 oz (75g) raw cane sugar
2 eggs, beaten
6 oz (175g) wholemeal flour
2 oz (50g) carob powder
1½ level teaspoonsful baking powder
1 tablespoonful natural unsweetened yogurt
4 oz (100g) small seedless raisins

Cream the margarine and sugar together until light and fluffy. Add the beaten eggs a little at a time. Fold in the flour, carob powder and baking powder. Gently stir in the yogurt and raisins.

Put the mixture into a greased and lined 8 inch square baking tin, spreading evenly. Bake at 350°F/ 180°C (Gas Mark 4) for about 30-40 minutes until firm to the touch. When cool, cut into squares.

Carob Brownies
(Makes approximately 10)

2 oz (50g) polyunsaturated margarine
2 oz (50g) block carob
1 tablespoonful honey
4 oz (100g) wholemeal flour
1½ teaspoonsful baking powder
2 oz (50g) chopped walnuts
2 tablespoonsful natural unsweetened yogurt

Melt the carob and margarine in a pan over a low heat. Remove from the heat and stir in the honey.

Put the flour, baking powder and walnuts into a mixing bowl. Stir in the yogurt. Lastly add the carob mixture and beat all the ingredients thoroughly. Pour the mixture into a greased and lined 8 inch square tin and bake for about 30-40 minutes at 350°F/180°C (Gas Mark 4). When cool, cut into squares.

Carob Madeleines
(Makes approximately 12-15)

4 oz (100g) polyunsaturated margarine
3 oz (75g) raw cane sugar
2 eggs, beaten
4 oz (100g) wholemeal flour
1 oz (25g) carob powder
1 tablespoonful natural unsweetened yogurt
1½ level teaspoonsful baking powder

For decoration
2 oz (50g) desiccated coconut
clear honey
halved glacé cherries

Cream the margarine and sugar together until light and fluffy. Add the beaten eggs a little at a time. Fold in the flour, carob powder, baking powder and yogurt.

Spoon the mixture into well greased *dariole* moulds, allowing room for the madeleines to rise whilst baking. Put the moulds on a baking tray and bake for about 20 minutes at 375°F/190°C (Gas Mark 5). To make sure that the madeleines are thoroughly cooked, test with a thin skewer whilst still in the oven. If the skewer comes out clean, the cakes are cooked through. When cooled, coat the madeleines in clear honey and then roll in desiccated coconut. Top with half a *glacé* cherry.

Carob Honey Squares

(Makes approximately 10 squares)

6 oz (175g) wholemeal flour
2 oz (50g) carob powder
2 level teaspoonsful baking powder
2 oz (50g) sultanas
3 tablespoonsful safflower oil
2 tablespoonsful clear honey
2 tablespoonsful natural unsweetened yogurt
little milk to mix

Put the flour, carob powder, baking powder and sultanas into a large mixing bowl. Stir in the safflower oil, honey and yogurt with enough milk to give a fairly runny consistency.

Pour the mixture into a greased and lined 8 inch square cake tin and bake for about 30 minutes at 350°F/180°C (Gas Mark 4). When cool, cut the cake into squares.

Carob Meringues
(Makes approximately 8 complete meringues)

4 eggs whites
8 oz (225g) raw cane sugar
4 oz (100g) carob powder
small carton fresh cream, whipped (for filling)

Whisk the egg whites until very stiff. Add the carob powder and half the sugar and whisk again. Fold in the remaining sugar.

Pipe small meringue swirls onto baking trays lined with waxed paper or greased greaseproof paper. Bake in a cool oven, 250°F/130°C (Gas Mark ¼) for several hours until crisp and dry. When cool, sandwich the meringue swirls together with whipped cream and serve as soon as possible before the meringues lose their crispness.

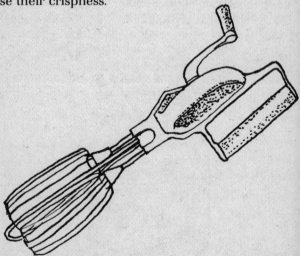

Carob Florentines
(Makes approximately 12-15)

4 oz (100g) polyunsaturated margarine
4 oz (100g) raw cane sugar
2 oz (50g) chopped blanched almonds
1 oz (25g) flaked almonds
1 oz (25g) chopped sultanas
1 oz (25g) mixed peel
1 oz (25g) chopped glacé cherries
1 tablespoonsful natural unsweetened yogurt
6 oz (175g) block carob

Line three baking trays with non-stick paper.

Melt the margarine in a pan over a low heat. Add the sugar and bring slowly to the boil. Boil for about one minute. Remove from the heat, allow to cool a little and stir in the almonds, sultanas, mixed peel and *glacé* cherries. Lastly, stir in the yogurt.

Drop small heaps of the mixture onto the baking trays and flatten slightly with a palette knife. Space the mixture well apart in order to allow for spreading during cooking. Bake for about 10 minutes at 350°F/180°C (Gas Mark 4), until golden brown. Allow to cool and lift off carefully with a palette knife.

Melt the carob in a bowl over hot water and spread over the smooth side of the florentines. When the carob has set a little, mark lines across with a fork to make a swirly pattern.

Carob Raisin Bars
(Makes 12-15)

3 oz (75g) polyunsaturated margarine
2 oz (50g) raw cane sugar
1 egg, beaten
2 tablespoonsful clear honey
6 oz (175g) wholemeal flour
1 oz (25g) carob powder
2 level teaspoonsful baking powder
1 tablespoonful natural unsweetened yogurt
4 oz (100g) raisins

Cream the margarine and sugar together until light and fluffy. Gradually add the beaten egg and then stir in the honey. Fold in the flour, carob powder and baking powder and lastly stir in the yogurt and raisins.

Spoon the mixture into a well greased shallow baking tin and bake for about 30-35 minutes at 350°F/180°C (Gas Mark 4). When cool, cut into bars before removing from the baking tin.

Carob Almond Slices
(Makes approximately 15-18 slices)

4 oz (100g) polyunsaturated margarine
2 oz (50g) raw cane sugar
6 oz (175g) wholemeal flour
2 oz (50g) carob powder
1 beaten egg for glazing
2 oz (50g) flaked almonds

Cream the margarine and sugar together until light

and fluffy. Fold in the flour and carob powder. Blend all the ingredients together well to form a fairly stiff mixture.

Press the mixture into a well-greased swiss roll tin and flatten evenly with a palette knife. Brush with beaten egg to glaze, and sprinkle with the flaked almonds.

Bake for about 20 minutes at 350°F/180°C (Gas Mark 4) until the biscuit mixture is crisp and the almonds are nicely browned.

So that the biscuits don't crumble or break, cut into slices whilst still warm but leave in the baking tin to cool thoroughly.

Carob Macaroons
(Makes approximately 10)

1 egg white
2 oz (50g) ground almonds
1 oz (25g) carob powder
1 oz (25g) raw cane sugar
½ teaspoonful almond essence
whole blanched almonds

Whisk the egg white until stiff. Fold in the ground almonds, carob powder, sugar and almond essence.

Put spoonsful of the mixture onto baking sheets lined with rice paper or non-stick paper, allowing for the mixture to spread during cooking. Place a whole blanched almond in the centre of each macaroon.

Bake for about 20-25 minutes at 350°F/180°C (Gas Mark 4) until firm.

Carob Cream Shells
(Makes approximately 10)

4 oz (100g) polyunsaturated margarine
4 oz (100g) raw cane sugar
1 egg, beaten
6 oz (175g) wholemeal flour
1 tablespoonful carob powder
fresh whipped cream (for filling)

Cream the margarine and sugar together until light and fluffy. Gradually add the beaten egg. Fold in the flour and carob powder.

Spread the mixture evenly into greased shell-shaped moulds or, using a forcing bag with a large star nozzle, pipe small shell shapes onto a greased baking tray.

Bake at 375°F/190°C (Gas Mark 5) for about 15 minutes. When cool, sandwich the shells together with fresh whipped cream.

Carob Peanut Cookies
(Makes approximately 15-20)

4 oz (100g) polyunsaturated margarine
2 oz (50g) raw cane sugar
6 oz (175g) wholemeal flour
2 oz (50g) carob powder
1 beaten egg to glaze
2 oz (50g) chopped shelled peanuts

Cream the margarine and sugar together until light and fluffy. Fold in the flour and carob powder to make a fairly stiff dough. Roll out the mixture on a floured board to about ¼-inch in thickness. Cut into rounds with a medium sized fluted cutter and place on a well-greased baking tray.

Glaze the biscuits with beaten egg and sprinkle with the chopped peanuts. Bake for about 12-15 minutes at 350°F/180°C (Gas Mark 4) until the biscuits are crisp and the peanuts are nicely browned.

Carob Bourbons
(Makes 6 complete biscuits)

4 oz (100g) polyunsaturated margarine
2 oz (50g) raw cane sugar
1 dessertspoonful natural unsweetened yogurt
5 oz (150g) wholemeal flour
1 oz (25g) carob powder
3 oz (75g) block carob (for filling)

Cream the margarine and sugar together thoroughly and then add the yogurt. Fold in the flour and carob powder – the mixture should be fairly stiff.

Roll the mixture out fairly thinly and cut into rectangles measuring approximately 3 inches by 1 inch. Put onto a well-greased baking tray and prick each biscuit with a fork. Bake for about 10-12 minutes at 350°F/180°C (Gas Mark 4).

Lift the biscuits off the baking tray carefully with a spatula and leave to cool on a wire rack. Melt the carob in a bowl over a pan of hot water. Sandwich the biscuits together with the melted carob.

Carob Fruit and Nut Cookies
(Makes approximately 15-20)

3 oz (75g) polyunsaturated margarine
2 oz (50g) raw cane sugar
1 egg, beaten
6 oz (175g) wholemeal flour
1 oz (25g) carob powder
1 level teaspoonful baking powder
2 oz (50g) almond nibs
2 oz (50g) raisins

Cream the margarine and sugar together thoroughly
and then gradually add the beaten egg. Fold in the
flour, carob powder and baking powder and then add
the almond nibs and raisins.

Drop spoonsful of the mixture onto well-greased
baking trays, allowing room for the biscuits to spread
whilst baking. Bake for about 12-15 minutes at 350°F/
180°C (Gas Mark 4).

Carob Chip Biscuits
(Makes approximately 25 biscuits)

4 oz (100g) polyunsaturated margarine
4 oz (100g) raw cane sugar
1 egg, beaten
8 oz (225g) wholemeal flour
1 level teaspoonful baking powder
8 oz (225g) carob chips

Cream the margarine and sugar together until light and fluffy. Add the beaten egg a little at a time. Fold in the flour and baking powder. Lastly add the carob chips.

Spoon small amounts of the mixture onto greased baking trays and bake for about 12 minutes at 375°F/190°C (Gas Mark 4).

Carob and Almond Biscuits
(Makes approximately 15-20 biscuits)

4 oz (100g) wholemeal flour
2 oz (50g) carob powder
2 oz (50g) ground almonds
4 oz (100g) polyunsaturated margarine
1 oz (25g) blanched almond nibs
1 tablespoonful clear honey
1 tablespoonful natural unsweetened yogurt

Put the flour, carob powder and ground almonds into a large mixing bowl and rub in the margarine until the mixture resembles fine breadcrumbs. Add the blanched almond nibs and then stir in the honey and yogurt.

Roll the mixture out thinly on a floured board and cut into rounds with a scone cutter. Place on a well-greased baking tray and bake for about 15 minutes at 350°F/180°C (Gas Mark 4).

Carob Coated Digestive Biscuits
(Makes approximately 15-20 biscuits)

8 oz (225g) wholemeal flour
4 oz (100g) polyunsaturated margarine
2 oz (50g) raw cane sugar
1 egg, beaten
2 tablespoonsful natural unsweetened yogurt
1 tablespoonful clear honey

For coating
4 oz (100g) block carob
1 dessertspoonful milk

Put the wholemeal flour into a large mixing bowl and rub in the margarine until the mixture resembles fine breadcrumbs. Mix in the sugar, egg, yogurt and honey, blending all the ingredients together well.

Roll out on a floured board and cut into 2 inch rounds with a plain cutter. Place on a well-greased baking tray and bake for about 25 minutes at 350°F/ 180°C (Gas Mark 4).

Whilst the biscuits are cooling, melt the block carob in a bowl over a pan of hot water. When melted, stir in the milk and blend well. Coat each biscuit with the carob coating and leave to set.

Carob Coconut Cookies
(Makes approximately 10-12)

2 egg whites
3 oz (75g) raw cane sugar
2 oz (50g) carob powder
6 oz (175g) desiccated coconut
Halved glacé cherries (for decoration)

Whisk the egg whites until stiff. Add the sugar and whisk the mixture again until stiff. Carefully fold in the carob powder and coconut.

Put teaspoonsful of the mixture onto baking trays lined with rice paper or non-stick paper, leaving room for the cookies to spread whilst in the oven. Place half a *glacé* cherry on each cookie and bake for about 40 minutes at 300°F/150°C (Gas Mark 2) until firm to the touch.

Carob Muesli Bites
(Makes approximately 15-18)

4 oz (100g) block carob
1 tablespoonful clear honey
2 oz (50g) polyunsaturated margarine
6 oz (175g) muesli
2 oz (50g) almond nibs

Break the carob into pieces and melt in a pan with the margarine over a gentle heat. When melted, remove from the heat and stir in the honey. Lastly add the muesli and almond nibs, mixing well.

Drop spoonsful of the mixture into small fluted paper cases and leave in the refrigerator to set.

Carob Orange Biscuits
(Makes approximately 15-20)

4 oz (100g) wholemeal flour
2 oz (50g) carob powder
2 oz (50g) raw cane sugar
4 oz (100g) polyunsaturated margarine
2 tablespoonsful natural unsweetened yogurt
grated rind of 1 orange
pure orange juice

Place the flour, carob powder, baking powder and sugar into a mixing bowl. Rub in the margarine until the mixture resembles fine breadcrumbs. Add the grated orange rind and enough orange juice to make a stiff dough.

Roll out thinly on a floured board and cut into rounds with a scone cutter. Bake for about 12-15 minutes at 350°F/180°C (Gas Mark 4).

Carob Rolled Oat Slices

(Makes approximately 10 slices)

4 oz (100g) block carob
4 oz (100g) polyunsaturated margarine
1 tablespoonful clear honey
8 oz (225g) rolled oats
2 oz (50g) desiccated coconut

Break the carob into pieces and place in a saucepan. Add the margarine and honey and melt together over a gentle heat. Remove from the heat and add the rolled oats and coconut, mixing thoroughly.

Spread the mixture evenly onto a greased shallow baking tin and bake for about 20-25 minutes at 350°F/180°C (Gas Mark 4). Leave to cool a little while and whilst still in the baking tin, cut into individual slices. Remove from the tin when completely cooled.

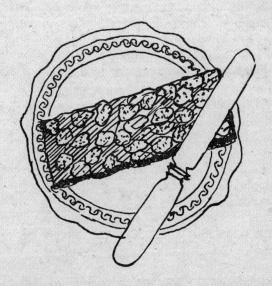

2. HOT PUDDINGS

Hot puddings are traditional, ever-popular family favourites. But as a natural-food minded cook you may feel dubious about incorporating puddings into a healthy eating programme. Prepared with natural, unrefined ingredients they are, however, a warming and nutritious end to a meal on a cold winter's night.

Steamed carob puddings will undoubtedly become a firm favourite with your family. They are full of flavour and goodness and are particularly delicious served with honey custard or natural yogurt.

Steamed Carob Pudding

(Serves 4)

4 oz (100g) polyunsaturated margarine
2 oz (50g) raw cane sugar
2 eggs, beaten
4 oz (100g) wholemeal flour
2 oz (50g) carob powder
2 level teaspoonsful baking powder
1 tablespoonful clear honey
1 tablespoonful natural unsweetened yogurt

Cream the margarine and sugar together until light
and fluffy. Slowly add the beaten eggs. Fold in the
flour, carob powder, baking powder, honey and
yogurt.

Spoon the mixture into a well-greased 1 pint
pudding basin. Cover with greaseproof paper or foil
and secure with string. Place in a steamer over a pan
of hot water, and steam for about 1½ hours.

Serve immediately with honey custard (see recipe
on page 59) or natural yogurt.

Carob Apple Pudding
(Serves 6)

1 lb (450g) cooking apples
3 tablespoonsful clear honey
grated rind of 1 lemon
3 oz (75g) polyunsaturated margarine
2 oz (50g) raw cane sugar
1 egg, beaten
2 tablespoonsful natural unsweetened yogurt
4 oz (100g) wholemeal flour
1 oz (25g) carob powder
2 level teaspoonsful baking powder

Peel and core the apples, then slice into a well-greased 1½ pint ovenproof pudding dish. Add the grated lemon rind to the apples and spread the honey on top.

Cream the margarine and sugar together until light and fluffy. Gradually add the beaten egg a little at a time. Fold in the flour, carob powder, baking powder and yogurt. Spoon the mixture onto the apples, spreading evenly.

Bake for about 40-45 minutes at 350°F/180°C (Gas Mark 4) and serve immediately with Honey Custard (see recipe on page 59).

Carob Almond Layer Pudding
(Serves 6)

4 oz (100g) polyunsaturated margarine
2 oz (50g) raw cane sugar
2 eggs, beaten
4 oz (100g) wholemeal flour
2 oz (50g) carob powder
2 level teaspoonsful baking powder
2 tablespoonsful clear honey
1 tablespoonful natural unsweetened yogurt
8 oz (225g) flaked almonds

Cream the margarine and sugar together until light and fluffy. Gradually add the beaten eggs a little at a time. Stir in one tablespoonful of clear honey and then fold in the flour, carob powder, baking powder and yogurt.

Grease a 1½ pint pudding basin and spoon the remaining tablespoonful of clear honey into the bottom. Place a layer of flaked almonds on top of the honey, followed by a layer of the pudding mixture. Carry on making up alternate layers of flaked almonds and pudding mixture.

Cover the basin with greaseproof paper or foil and secure. Place in a steamer and steam for about 1½ hours. Serve with Honey Custard (see recipe on page 59) or natural yogurt.

Carob Fig Pudding
(Serves 6)

6 oz (175g) dried figs (soaked overnight)
3 oz (75g) polyunsaturated margarine
2 oz (50g) raw cane sugar
grated rind of 1 lemon
2 oz (50g) wholemeal flour
2 oz (50g) carob powder
2 oz (50g) fresh wholemeal breadcrumbs
1 oz (25g) ground almonds
1½ level teaspoonsful baking powder
1 level teaspoonful mixed spice
3 tablespoonsful natural unsweetened yogurt
little milk to mix

Drain the figs, remove the stalks and cut into small pieces.

Cream the margarine, sugar and lemon rind together until light and fluffy. Fold in the flour, carob powder, breadcrumbs, almonds, figs, baking powder and mixed spice. Add the yogurt and enough milk to produce a soft dropping consistency.

Spoon the mixture into a well-greased 1-1¼ pint pudding basin, cover with foil and secure. Steam for about 2-3 hours and serve with Honey Custard (see recipe on page 59) or natural yogurt.

Carob Cherry Puddings
(Makes 6 individual puddings)

6 teaspoonsful clear honey
6 oz (175g) glacé cherries
3 oz (75g) polyunsaturated margarine
2 oz (50g) raw cane sugar
1 egg, beaten
3 oz (75g) wholemeal flour
1 oz (25g) carob powder
1½ level teaspoonsful baking powder
2 tablespoonsful natural unsweetened yogurt

Put 1 teaspoonful of clear honey in the bottom of each of six well-greased individual *dariole* moulds. Place three halved *glacé* cherries in each mould on top of the honey, with the flat side uppermost. Chop the remaining cherries into quarters and reserve.

Cream the margarine and sugar together until light and fluffy, and then gradually add the beaten egg. Fold in the flour, carob powder, baking powder and remaining cherries. Stir in the yogurt.

Divide the mixture between the *dariole* moulds, allowing room for the puddings to rise during steaming. Cover each mould with foil and secure. Steam the puddings for approximately 1 hour and serve immediately with Honey Custard (see recipe on page 59).

Carob Pear Pudding
(Serves 4)

2 eggs
2 oz (50g) raw cane sugar
4 oz (100g) wholemeal flour
1 oz (25g) carob powder
2 level teaspoonsful baking powder
2 tablespoonsful natural unsweetened yogurt
1 lb (450g) dessert pears
2 oz (50g) flaked almonds

Put the eggs and sugar in a large mixing bowl and stand it in a sink of hot water. Whisk together until the mixture is thick and creamy and leaves a trail when the whisk is removed. Carefully fold in the flour, carob powder, baking powder and yogurt.

Peel the pears and slice into a greased ovenproof serving dish. Pour the carob mixture on top of the pears and spread evenly with a palette knife. Sprinkle with flaked almonds.

Bake for 30-35 minutes at 375°F/190°C (Gas Mark 5) until the top of the pudding is firm to the touch and the almonds are nicely browned. Serve hot with Honey Custard (see recipe on page 59).

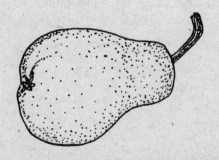

Carob Spotted Dick

(Serves 4-6)

6 oz (175g) wholemeal flour
2 oz (50g) carob powder
2 level teaspoonsful baking powder
4 oz (100g) polyunsaturated margarine
6 oz (175g) currants
1 egg, beaten
2 tablespoonsful clear honey
2 tablespoonsful natural unsweetened yogurt
little milk to mix

Put the flour, carob powder and baking powder into a mixing bowl. Rub in the margarine until the mixture resembles fine breadcrumbs. Stir in the currants.

Make a well in the centre of the dry ingredients and mix in the beaten egg, honey and yogurt. Add a little milk to produce a dropping consistency.

Spoon the mixture into a well greased 1½ pint pudding basin, cover with greaseproof paper or foil and secure with string. Steam for about 1½ hours and serve with Honey Custard (see recipe on page 59) or natural yogurt.

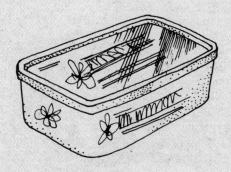

Carob Buttermilk Pudding
(Serves 6)

4 oz (100g) polyunsaturated margarine
2 oz (50g) raw cane sugar
1 egg, beaten
1 tablespoonful clear honey
5 oz (150g) wholemeal flour
2 oz (50g) carob powder
2 level teaspoonsful baking powder
2 tablespoonsful buttermilk

Cream the margarine and sugar together until light and fluffy. Add the beaten egg a little at a time. Stir in the clear honey and then fold in the flour, carob powder and baking powder. Lastly, fold in the buttermilk.

Spoon the mixture into a greased 1½ pint pudding basin, cover with greaseproof paper or foil and secure with string. Steam for about 1½ hours and serve hot with Honey Custard (see recipe on page 59).

Carob Pineapple Upside-Down Pudding
(Serves 6)

1 small fresh pineapple
1 oz (25g) glacé cherries
2 tablespoonsful clear honey
4 oz (100g) polyunsaturated margarine
3 oz (75g) raw cane sugar
2 eggs, beaten
4 oz (100g) wholemeal flour
2 oz (50g) carob powder
2 tablespoonsful natural unsweetened yogurt
2 level teaspoonsful baking powder
little milk to mix

Peel and slice the fresh pineapple into rings, cutting
out the centre core. Well-grease an 8 inch round cake
tin and spread the clear honey over the bottom.
Arrange the pineapple slices on top of the layer of
honey and place a *glacé* cherry in each centre core
hole.

Cream the margarine and sugar together until light
and fluffy. Gradually add the beaten eggs. Fold in the
flour, carob powder, baking powder and yogurt. If
necessary add a little milk to give a dropping consistency.

Spread the mixture on top of the pineapple rings
and bake at 350°F/180°C (Gas Mark 4) for about 40-45
minutes, until the top of the cake is firm to the touch.
Carefully turn out the cake onto a round serving dish
and serve hot with Honey Custard (see recipe on page
59).

Carob Orange Layer Puddings
(Makes 6 individual puddings)

4 oz (100g) polyunsaturated margarine
4 oz (100g) raw cane sugar
2 eggs, beaten
5 oz (150g) wholemeal flour
2 level teaspoonsful baking powder
1 tablespoonful natural unsweetened yogurt
1 oz (25g) carob powder
grated rind of one orange
2 teaspoonsful pure orange juice
6 teaspoonsful raw cane sugar marmalade

Cream the margarine and sugar together until light and fluffy. Gradually add the beaten eggs a little at a time. Fold in the flour, baking powder and yogurt. Divide the mixture into two equal parts. Add the carob powder to one half and the orange rind and juice to the remaining half.

Put a teaspoonful of raw cane sugar marmalade in the bottom of six well-greased *dariole* moulds. Spoon the pudding mixture in alternate layers into each mould, allowing for the puddings to rise during steaming. Cover each mould with greaseproof paper or foil and secure. Steam for about 1 hour and serve immediately with Honey Custard (see recipe on page 59) or natural yogurt.

Carob Brown Rice Pudding

2 oz (50g) brown rice
1 pint milk
3 tablespoonsful clear honey
2 oz (50g) grated block carob

Wash the brown rice and put into a greased 1½ pint pudding dish. Pour the milk onto the rice and stir in the honey. Bake at 300°F/150°C (Gas Mark 2) for 2-3 hours.

When the pudding has been in the oven for 1 hour, stir in the grated block carob. Test the rice to make sure that it is soft before serving because brown rice takes longer to cook than the white polished variety.

Honey Custard

½ pint (275ml) milk
2 tablespoonsful clear honey
1 vanilla pod
2 egg yolks

Split the vanilla pod lengthways. Place in a pan with the milk, and heat. Remove from the heat and leave to infuse for 10 minutes with a lid on the pan. Then remove the vanilla pod and stir in the honey.

Whisk the egg yolks in a large mixing bowl. Re-heat the milk to boiling point and pour over the egg yolks, stirring continuously. Return the mixture to the pan and stir continuously over a low heat until the custard thickens and becomes creamy. Serve immediately over hot puddings.

3. SPECIAL OCCASION DESSERTS

A natural-food dinner party or special occasion meal is not always easy to plan. You probably don't want to stray from your wholefood principles but at the same time you may be afraid that your guests will think of you as a 'health food nut'. As wholefoods grow in popularity, however, natural-food dinner parties are becoming more and more acceptable and are often greatly appreciated by the guests, and the hosts are no longer considered faddish, as they would have been some years ago.

The choice of dessert may be the most difficult part of planning a natural-food dinner party, particularly as special occasion desserts don't normally conjure up the image of nutritious food. Make lavish use of fresh fruits and, wherever possible, use natural yogurt instead of cream. Unfortunately, yogurt does not whip so in some cases it may be necessary to use fresh cream for whipping and decoration. Needless to say, carob should always be used in place of chocolate or cocoa powder and if you are worried about what your guests may think of this often unheard of alternative, rest assured that they will be delighted when you tell them that at last they can eat a chocolate taste-alike without feeling those familiar pangs of guilt.

Carob Tropical Fruit Pavlova
(Serves 6-8)

5 egg whites
8 oz (225g) raw cane sugar
5 oz (150g) carob powder

For filling
½ pint (275ml) natural unsweetened yogurt
2 tablespoonsful clear honey
1 banana, peeled
1 fresh mango, skinned
2 oz (50g) fresh strawberries
2 oz (50g) black grapes, pips removed
half a small fresh pineapple, peeled
1 small orange, peeled

Draw a 9 inch circle on a piece of greaseproof paper. Grease the circle thoroughly and place on a baking tray.

Whisk the egg whites until very stiff. Whisk in the carob powder and half of the raw cane sugar. Fold in the remaining sugar. Spoon the meringue mixture onto the circle and spread evenly with a palette knife.

Bake at 250°F/130°C (Gas Mark ¼) for several hours until the meringue is crisp and dry.

Stir the honey into the yogurt. Cut all the fresh fruit into small pieces and fold into this mixture. Pile the yogurt and fruit mixture onto the meringue circle and serve immediately.

Carob Pears Belle Hélène
(Serves 4)

4 ripe pears
1 vanilla pod, split
4 oz (100g) raw cane sugar
1 pint (550ml) water
2 oz (50g) almond nibs (for decoration)

For carob sauce
6 oz (175g) block carob
2 tablespoonsful natural unsweetened yogurt
or buttermilk

Peel and core the pears and leave to one side.

Place the sugar and water in a pan and boil rapidly for about 2 minutes until syrup begins to form. Place the pears and the vanilla pod in the syrup mixture and poach for about 10 minutes over a low heat. Leave the pears to cool in the syrup.

To make the sauce, break the carob into pieces and melt in a bowl over a pan of hot water. When fully melted, stir in the yogurt or buttermilk and blend together well.

Drain the pears and coat with the carob sauce. Sprinkle with almond nibs and serve immediately.

Carob Hazelnut Meringue Gâteau
(Makes a 3 layer 7 inch meringue)

6 egg whites
10 oz (275g) raw cane sugar
6 oz (175g) carob powder
8 oz (225g) chopped hazelnuts
½ pint (275ml) natural yogurt
2 tablespoonsful clear honey
grated block carob (for decoration)

Draw three 7 inch diameter circles on greaseproof paper. Grease the circles well and place on baking trays.

Whisk the egg whites until stiff. Add the carob powder and half of the sugar and whisk again. Fold in the remaining half of the sugar. Pipe the meringue onto the three marked circles. If necessary, spread out evenly with a palette knife.

Bake in a cool oven, 250°F/130°C (Gas Mark ¼) for 2-3 hours until the meringue is crisp and dry. Remove carefully from the greaseproof paper and leave to cool.

Stir the honey into the yogurt and fold in the chopped hazelnuts. Reserve ⅓ of the hazelnut and yogurt mixture. Sandwich the meringue layers together with the remaining part.

Spread the reserved hazelnut and yogurt mixture on top of the meringue and sprinkle with grated block carob.

Carob Pots de Crème
(Serves 6)

6 oz (175g) block carob
¾ pint (425ml) milk
1 oz (25g) raw cane sugar
4 egg yolks
1 tablespoonful dark rum

For decoration
whipped cream
grated block carob

Put the milk to warm in a pan over a gentle heat.

Melt the carob in a bowl over a pan of hot water, remove from the heat when fully melted and stir in the sugar and the rum. Add the egg yolks to the mixture one at a time, mixing very thoroughly. Add the warmed milk, stirring continuously. Strain into individual ramekin dishes.

Place the dishes in a roasting tin filled with approximately 1 inch of cold water and bake for about 30 minutes at 325°F/170°C (Gas Mark 3) until visibly set.

After taking out of the oven, leave to cool for a little while and then refrigerate for about 1 hour in order to chill. Before serving, decorate with piped whipped cream and sprinkle with grated block carob.

Apple Meringues with Carob Sauce
(Serves 4)

4 large dessert apples
syrup made with 1 pint water and
4 oz (100g) raw cane sugar
1 vanilla pod
flaked almonds (for decoration)

For meringue
2 egg whites
4 oz (100g) raw cane sugar

For carob sauce
4 oz (100g) block carob
2 tablespoonsful natural unsweetened yogurt
or buttermilk

Put the sugar and water into a pan and boil rapidly for about 2 minutes until syrup begins to form. Split the vanilla pod lengthways and add to the syrup.

Peel and core the apples, put into the pan with the syrup and poach over a gentle heat for about 15 minutes until the fruit is tender. Put the apples in an ovenproof dish.

To make the meringue, whisk the egg whites until stiff. Add half the sugar, whisk again and then fold in the remaining sugar with a spoon. Pipe the meringue over each apple, covering completely and bake for about 15-20 minutes at 300°F/150°C (Gas Mark 2) until golden brown.

To make the sauce, break the carob into pieces and melt in a bowl over a pan of hot water. Remove from the heat and stir in the yogurt or buttermilk. Pour the sauce over the apple meringues, sprinkle with flaked almonds and serve immediately.

Carob Nut Sundae
(Serves 2)

**4 scoops carob ice cream (see recipe on page
   74)**
2 tablespoonsful natural yogurt
2 oz (50g) flaked almonds

For sauce
2 oz (50g) block carob
1 tablespoonful natural yogurt or buttermilk

To make the sauce, melt the carob in a bowl over hot
water. When melted, stir in the yogurt or buttermilk.
   Place two scoops of carob ice cream in each
sundae glass and top with a tablespoonful of natural
yogurt.
   Pour the cooled carob sauce over the ice cream and
yogurt and sprinkle with flaked almonds.

Carob Calypso Sundae
(Serves 2)

**4 scoops carob ice cream
   (see recipe on page 74)**
2 measures Tia Maria Liqueur
2 tablespoonsful natural yogurt
2 oz (50g) flaked almonds

Put two scoops of carob ice cream in each sundae
glass. Pour a measure of Tia Maria over the ice cream.
Top with yogurt and sprinkle with flaked almonds.

Carob Pineapple Gâteau
(Serves 6-8)

6 oz (175g) polyunsaturated margarine
4 oz (100g) raw cane sugar
3 eggs, beaten
4 oz (100g) wholemeal flour
2 oz (50g) carob powder
2 level teaspoonsful baking powder
1 small fresh pineapple
½ pint (275ml) natural unsweetened yogurt
2 tablespoonsful clear honey
2 oz (50g) flaked almonds (for decoration)

Cream the margarine and sugar together until light and fluffy. Gradually add the beaten eggs a little at a time. Fold in the flour, carob powder and baking powder. Spoon the mixture into a greased and lined rectangular baking tin (12 x 8 inches).

Bake at 375°F/190°C (Gas Mark 5) for about 20-25 minutes until the cake is firm to the touch.

Whilst the cake is cooling, peel the fresh pineapple, cut into slices, remove the centre core and chop into small pieces. Stir the honey into the yogurt and fold in the fresh chopped pineapple.

Remove the crusty edges from the cake and divide into three equal parts. Sandwich the cake together with the pineapple and yogurt mixture and pile the remainder on top of the cake. Sprinkle with flaked almonds.

Carob and Cream Mousse
(Serves 4)

3 oz (75g) block carob
3 eggs, separated
¼ pint (150ml) whipped double cream
1 tablespoonful dark rum
blanched almonds (for decoration)

Melt the carob in a bowl over a pan of hot water. Remove from the heat and stir in the egg yolks. Add the rum and fold in the whipped cream. Whisk the egg whites stiffly and fold into the carob mixture.

Divide into individual glasses and leave to set in the refrigerator for 2-3 hours. Decorate with piped whipped cream and chopped blanched almonds.

Variation:
For a less rich dessert that is suitable for children, simply omit the cream and the rum, following the same procedure.

Carob Raspberry Box
(Serves 6-8)

3 eggs
3 oz (75g) raw cane sugar
6 oz (175g) wholemeal flour
2 level teaspoonsful baking powder
1 tablespoonful hot water

For filling and decoration
6 oz (175g) block carob
1 lb (450g) fresh raspberries

½ pint (275ml) natural unsweetened yogurt
3 tablespoonsful clear honey
carob leaves (see page 75)

Put the eggs and sugar together in a large mixing bowl. Stand it in a sink of hot water and whisk the contents together until thick and creamy. Remove the bowl from the hot water and carefully fold in the flour and baking powder. Stir in the hot water. Pour the mixture into a greased and lined 8 inch square cake tin. Bake for about 30 minutes at 350°F/180°C (Gas Mark 4) until the cake is well-risen and firm to the touch.

Whilst the cake is baking, melt the carob in a bowl over hot water. When completely melted, spread fairly thickly and evenly onto a large piece of non-stick paper. When the carob is almost set, mark into 1½ inch squares with a sharp knife. Peel off from the paper when the squares have hardened. Reserve 12 whole raspberries for decoration and mix the rest with the yogurt and 2 tablespoonsful of honey.

When the cake has cooled, coat the sides with clear honey. Press the carob squares around the sides of the cake to make a box. You will need two rows of squares which should be slightly overlapping. The top row of squares should be above the top level of the cake. Pile the yogurt and raspberry mixture on top of the cake, spreading evenly. Decorate with the reserved raspberries and carob leaves.

Variation:
For an extra special dessert, sprinkle the cake with sherry or cherry brandy before decorating with the yogurt and raspberries.

Carob Strawberry Gâteau
(Makes 8 inch gâteau)

4 eggs
4 oz (100g) raw cane sugar
6 oz (175g) wholemeal flour
2 oz (50g) carob powder
3 level teaspoonsful baking powder
1 tablespoonful hot water
**small amount of fresh whipped cream (for
      decoration)**

For filling
½ pint (275ml) natural yogurt
1 lb (450g) fresh strawberries
1 tablespoonful raw cane sugar

Put the eggs and sugar into a large mixing bowl, stand it in a sink of hot water and whisk until thick and creamy. The whisk should leave a trail when you take it out of the mixture. Carefully fold in the flour, carob powder and baking powder. Add the hot water. Place the mixture into a greased and lined 8 inch cake tin and bake for about 35-40 minutes at 350°F/180°C (Gas Mark 4) until firm to the touch.

Whilst the cake is in the oven, wash the strawberries and sprinkle with the raw cane sugar. Allow the sugar to soak in for about 10 minutes. Reserve about 12 strawberries for decoration. Slice the remaining strawberries into quarters and fold into the yogurt.

When the cake is cool, cut into three slices. Sandwich the layers with the strawberry and yogurt mixture. Cut the reserved strawberries in half and arrange on top of the gâteau. Put the whipped cream into a piping bag with a ¼-inch star nozzle and pipe around the strawberries.

4. CHILDREN'S PARTY RECIPES

Children's parties in particular can be a problem to wholefood-minded mothers. How to prepare something that is pleasing to the child's eye, tastes delicious and is nutritious at the same time? A difficult task, you may say, but with a little effort and imagination, a children's party can turn into a wholefooder's delight.

Older children especially may often feel rebellious towards a natural-food party, worried about what their friends might think about your wholefood concoctions. And yet having read about the harmful ingredients and refined sugar contained in chocolate, in all probability you naturally want to steer clear of overloading their systems with chocolate cakes, chocolate biscuits and so forth.

From the sweets and treats aspect, carob is the perfect answer to your problems. Children will find it difficult to resist this chocolate look-alike and taste-alike and will almost certainly not be able to tell the difference.

Basic Mixture for Carob Fancy Cakes
(Makes approximately 12-15)

4 oz (100g) polyunsaturated margarine
3 oz (75g) raw cane sugar
2 eggs, beaten
1 tablespoonful natural unsweetened yogurt
4 oz (100g) wholemeal flour
1 oz (25g) carob powder
1½ level teaspoonsful baking powder
little milk to mix

Cream the margarine and sugar together until light and fluffy. Gradually add the beaten eggs, then fold in the yogurt, flour, carob powder and baking powder. If necessary, add a little milk to produce a dropping consistency.

Spoon the mixture into individual paper cases and bake for about 12-15 minutes at 350°F/180°C (Gas Mark 4) until firm to the touch.

Carob Butterflies

Make a batch of cakes using the mixture above. When cool, slice the top off each cake with a sharp knife and cut the top in half. Pipe whipped cream onto the centre of the cakes and replace the two halves on top to form butterfly wings.

Carob Kings and Queens
(Makes 2 Kings and 2 Queens)

6 oz (175g) polyunsaturated margarine
6 oz (175g) raw cane sugar
1 large egg, beaten
10 oz (275g) wholemeal flour
2 oz (50g) carob powder

For decoration
currants
almond nibs

For carob icing
2 oz (50g) block carob

Cream the margarine and sugar together until light and fluffy. Gradually add the beaten egg. Fold in the flour and carob powder. The mixture should be fairly stiff.

Roll out on a floured board to about ¼-inch thickness. Cut out Kings and Queens with specially shaped cutters or mark out and cut the shapes with a sharp knife. Decorate the shapes with currants for the eyes and almond nibs for the mouth and nose. Bake for about 10 minutes on a well greased baking tray at 350°F/180°C (Gas Mark 4).

To make the carob icing, break the carob into pieces and melt in a bowl over a pan of hot water. Remove the bowl from the water and leave the carob to cool a little. As it begins to set and thicken, place the carob into a piping bag and pipe immediately.

Decorate the Kings and Queens with the melted carob as you or your children like. For example, give them hair, buttons, waistcoats, skirts, etc.

Carob Top Hats

Make a batch of cakes using the mixture on page 72. Using a sharp knife, cut out the top centre part of the cake, without cutting too deeply. Fill the hollowed centre with whipped cream and replace the centre piece to form a top hat.

Carob Ice Cream
(Serves 6)

1 pint (550ml) milk
1 vanilla pod
4 egg yolks
3 oz (75g) raw cane sugar
3 oz (75g) block carob
½ pint (275ml) double cream, lightly whipped

Split the vanilla pod lengthways. Heat the milk and the vanilla pod together and leave to infuse for 15 minutes.

Whisk the egg yolks and sugar together.

Remove the vanilla pod and re-heat the milk. Add the hot milk to the whisked eggs and sugar, beating thoroughly.

Melt the carob in a bowl over a pan of hot water. When melted, add to the milk mixture and allow to cool a little. Lastly fold in the double cream and pour into a container suitable for freezing. Freeze until it begins to set around the edges and then pour into a bowl, beat well and return to freezing container. Freeze until solid.

If you are serving the ice cream alone, decorate with carob leaves (see page 75).

Carob Leaves

2 oz (50g) block carob

Melt the carob in a bowl over a pan of hot water. Spread fairly thickly onto waxed paper with a palette knife. When almost set, mark out leaf shapes with a sharp knife. When completely set, peel off the leaf shapes from the waxed paper.

Carob Banana Split
(Serves 4)

4 bananas
4 scoops carob ice cream (see page 74)
2 oz (50g) almond nibs

For carob sauce
4 oz (100g) block carob
2 tablespoonsful buttermilk

Make the carob sauce by melting the carob in a bowl over a pan of hot water. When completely melted, stir in the buttermilk. Peel the bananas and slice in half lengthways. Put the banana halves in individual serving dishes and sandwich together with one or two scoops of carob ice cream. Cover with the carob sauce and sprinkle with almond nibs. (For very young children, omit the almond nibs and decorate with carob leaves instead).

Carob Meringue Nests
(Makes approximately 10 nests)

2 egg whites
4 oz (100g) raw cane sugar
1 dessertspoonful carob powder

For filling
**4 oz (100g) fresh fruit (e.g. bananas,
    strawberries, oranges)**
¼ pint (150ml) natural unsweetened yogurt
1 tablespoonful clear honey

For decoration
marzipan eggs
chicks or robins

Put the egg whites into a mixing bowl and whisk until
very stiff. Add the carob powder and half the sugar
and whisk again. Fold in the remaining sugar. Put the
mixture into a piping bag fitted with a large star
nozzle. Pipe a small circle onto a greased baking tray
and then pipe another circle inside to form the
bottom of the nest. Pipe another circle on top of the
outer circle to form the wall of the nest. Bake the
nests for 2-3 hours in a cool oven, that is 250°F/130°C
(Gas Mark ¼) until they are crisp and dry.

Dice the fresh fruit into small pieces and mix into
the yogurt and clear honey. When the meringues
have cooled, fill in the centre of the nests with the
fruit and yogurt mixture.

Make small eggs out of marzipan and place three in
the centre of each nest, on top of the fruit and yogurt.
Place a small chick or robin at the side of the eggs.

Carob Wheat Flake Clusters
(Makes approximately 1 dozen)

8 oz (225g) block carob
4 oz (100g) whole wheat flakes
2 oz (50g) almond nibs

Mix the whole wheat flakes and almond nibs together.

Melt the carob in a bowl over a pan of hot water. Remove from the heat and stir the wheat flakes and almond nibs into the carob, making sure that the wheat flakes don't disintegrate.

Spoon the mixture onto waxed paper in clusters and leave to set. Serve in small fluted paper cases.

Carob Mousse
(Serves 4)

3 oz (75g) block carob
3 eggs, separated
grated block carob (for decoration)

Melt the carob in a bowl over a pan of hot water. Remove from the heat and stir in the egg yolks. Whisk the egg whites until stiff and fold into the carob mixture.

Spoon into individual sundae glasses and leave to set in the refrigerator for about 2 hours. Just before serving, sprinkle with grated block carob.

Carob Merry-Go-Round Cake
(Makes two layer 8 inch cake)

8 oz (225g) polyunsaturated margarine
6 oz (175g) raw cane sugar
3 eggs, beaten
1 tablespoonful clear honey
6 oz (175g) wholemeal flour
2 oz (50g) carob powder
3 level teaspoonsful baking powder
1 tablespoonful natural unsweetened yogurt

For filling and decoration
clear honey
6 oz (175g) block carob
long meat skewer
different coloured ribbons
animal biscuits (see page 79)
small amount of fresh whipped cream

Cream the margarine and sugar together until light and fluffy. Add the beaten eggs a little at a time. Stir in the clear honey and then fold in the flour, carob powder, baking powder and yogurt. Spoon the mixture into two greased and lined 8 inch round cake tins and bake for about 25 minutes at 375°F/190°C, (Gas Mark 5) until the cakes are firm to the touch. When cool, sandwich the cakes together with honey.

Melt the carob in a bowl over a pan of hot water and spread evenly over the top and sides of the cake. Before the carob coating sets, place plain animal biscuits around the sides of the cake.

Cover a meat skewer with different coloured ribbons, allowing each piece of ribbon to overhang by about 12 inches from the top of the skewer so that

the ribbons can fall over the cake to make the merry-
go-round. You should have the same number of
ribbons as animal biscuits. Place the skewer firmly
into the centre of the cake, giving each animal a piece
of the ribbon. Decorate the top of the cake with a little
piped whipped cream.

Carob Coated Animal Biscuits
(Makes approximately 15-20)

8 oz (225g) wholemeal flour
3 oz (75g) raw cane sugar
4 oz (100g) polyunsaturated margarine
1 egg, beaten
1 tablespoonful natural unsweetened yogurt

For coating and decoration
8 oz (225g) block carob
seedless raisins
glacé cherries

Put the flour and sugar into a large mixing bowl and
rub in the margarine until the mixture resembles fine
breadcrumbs. Mix in the beaten egg and enough
yogurt to form a stiff dough. Roll out to about ¼-inch
thickness and cut into animal shapes with animal
cutters. Place on a well-greased baking tray and bake
for about 15 minutes at 350°F/180°C (Gas Mark 4).

Melt the block carob in a bowl over a pan of hot
water. When the biscuits are cool, coat each one with
the melted carob. Decorate the animals with raisins
and small pieces of *glacé* cherries to make the eyes
and mouths.

Carob Owls

(Makes approximately 1 dozen)

4 oz (100g) polyunsaturated margarine
3 oz (75g) raw cane sugar
2 eggs, beaten
4 oz (100g) wholemeal flour
1 oz (25g) carob powder
1½ level teaspoonsful baking powder

For decoration
3 tablespoonsful clear honey
4 oz (100g) desiccated coconut
2 oz (50g) small seedless raisins
3 glacé cherries, cut into quarters

Cream the margarine and sugar together until light and fluffy. Gradually add the beaten eggs a little at a time. Fold in the flour, carob powder and baking powder. Spoon the mixture into well greased *dariole* moulds, allowing for the cakes to rise during baking. Place the moulds on a baking tray and bake for about 20 minutes at 375°F/180°C (Gas Mark 5).

When the cakes have cooled, coat each one with honey and roll in the desiccated coconut. To make the owl's eyes, stick two raisins onto the cakes with a little honey. Place a quarter *glacé* cherry slightly below the eyes to form the owl's beak.

Carob Banana Baskets
(Makes approximately 12-15)

4 oz (100g) polyunsaturated margarine
2 oz (50g) raw cane sugar
2 eggs, beaten
1 tablespoonful clear honey
4 oz (100g) wholemeal flour
1 oz (25g) carob powder
1½ level teaspoonsful baking powder
1 tablespoonful natural unsweetened yogurt

For decoration
2 bananas, peeled and sliced into rounds
clear honey
piece of angelica, approximately 6 inches
    in length

Cream the margarine and sugar together until light and fluffy. Gradually add the beaten eggs a little at a time. Stir in the honey and then fold in the flour, carob powder, baking powder and yogurt. Spoon small amounts of the mixture into small individual paper cases and bake for about 12-15 minutes at 350°F/180°C (Gas Mark 4). When the cakes have cooled, arrange slices of banana on top of each one and glaze with a little clear honey.

Soak the angelica in warm water to make it pliable. Cut it into thin slices and bend to form the shape of the basket handles. Stick the two ends of each piece of angelica into the cakes, making sure that the handles are firmly implanted.

Carob Meringue Boats
(Makes approximately 6-8 boats)

3 egg whites
6 oz (175g) raw cane sugar
3 oz (75g) carob powder

For decoration
small carton fresh cream, whipped
8 oz (225g) fresh strawberries
coloured paper/glue
wooden cocktail sticks

Whisk the egg whites until very stiff. Whisk in the carob powder and half of the sugar. Fold in the remaining sugar.

Using an icing bag with a large star nozzle, pipe oval boat shapes onto a baking tray lined with waxed or greased greaseproof paper. Bake for about 2 hours at 250°F/130°C (Gas Mark ¼) until the meringues are crisp and dry.

When cool, pipe fresh cream on top of each boat shape and decorate with whole strawberries. Make a sail or flag for the boats by sticking coloured paper onto cocktail sticks. Place a sail or flag in the centre strawberry on each boat. Serve as soon as possible whilst still crisp.

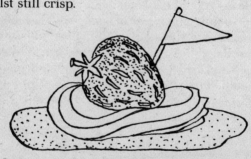

Carob Clock Cake

(Makes two layer 7 inch cake)

6 oz (175g) polyunsaturated margarine
4 oz (100g) raw cane sugar
2 eggs, beaten
5 oz (150g) wholemeal flour
2 oz (50g) carob powder
2 level teaspoonsful baking powder
2 tablespoonsful natural unsweetened yogurt

For filling and decoration
clear honey
4 oz (100g) block carob
little milk
angelica strips/half glacé cherry
small amount of fresh whipped cream

Cream the margarine and sugar together until light and fluffy. Add the beaten eggs a little at a time and then fold in the flour, carob powder, baking powder and yogurt. Spoon the mixture into two greased and lined 7 inch round cake tins. Bake for about 20-25 minutes at 375°F/190°C (Gas Mark 5) until the cakes are firm to the touch. When cool, sandwich the cakes together with clear honey.

Melt the carob in a bowl over a pan of hot water and add a little milk to make it smooth. Spoon on top of the cake and spread evenly.

Place the whipped cream into an icing bag fitted with a small, straight writing nozzle and pipe the clock numbers onto the cake. To make the clock hands, cut two strips of angelica. Place half a *glacé* cherry in the centre of the cake and place the clock hands in accordance with the child's age.

Carob Funny Faces
(Makes approximately 12-15)

4 oz (100g) polyunsaturated margarine
2 oz (50g) raw cane sugar
2 eggs, beaten
1 tablespoonful clear honey
4 oz (100g) wholemeal flour
1 oz (25g) carob powder
1½ level teaspoonsful baking powder
1 tablespoonful natural unsweetened yogurt

For decoration
8 oz (225g) block carob, melted over hot water
seedless raisins
glacé cherries, cut into quarters
almond nibs

Cream the margarine and sugar together until light and fluffy. Add the beaten eggs a little at a time. Stir in the honey and then fold in the flour, carob powder, baking powder and yogurt. Spoon the mixture into small paper cases and bake for about 12-15 minutes at 350°F/180°C (Gas Mark 4).

When cool, coat the cakes with melted carob, and decorate with raisins for the eyes, *glacé* cherry quarters for the nose, and almond nibs to form the mouth and eyebrows.

5. DRINKS

Long, cool summer drinks and hot, warming winter night-caps – delicious and nutritious for children and adults alike. Made with natural, additive-free ingredients, they are the perfect in-between-meal-filler and a nourishing dietary accompaniment for children, particularly those with poor appetites who eat little solid food at regular meal times.

Milk, natural yogurt, honey, carob and fresh fruits are the nutritive, vitamin-packed foods that are the basis of the following hot and cold drinks.

Carob Shake
(Serves 2)

½ pint (275ml) chilled milk
2 tablespoonsful natural unsweetened yogurt
2 teaspoonsful clear honey
1 tablespoonful carob powder
block carob to grate

Put all the ingredients into a blender and blend at high speed for about 20 seconds. Pour into tall glasses, sprinkle with grated block carob and serve immediately.

Carob and Banana Cooler
(Serves 2)

½ pint (275ml) chilled milk
1 banana
2 tablespoonsful natural unsweetened yogurt
2 teaspoonsful clear honey
2 scoops carob ice cream (see recipe on page 74)

Peel and slice the banana and place into a blender together with the milk, yogurt and honey. Blend for about 30 seconds. Pour into tall glasses, and top with a scoop of carob ice-cream. Serve immediately.

Spiced Carob Warmer
(Serves 2)

4 oz (100g) block carob
¾ pint (425ml) milk
2 teaspoonsful honey or raw cane sugar
¼ teaspoonful ground nutmeg
½ teaspoonful ground cinnamon

For topping
2 teaspoonsful natural yogurt
grated block carob

Melt the carob in a bowl over a pan of hot water. Heat the milk in a separate pan. When the carob has melted, stir into the warmed milk, together with the honey, nutmeg and cinnamon. Put the mixture into a blender and blend at high speed for about 20 seconds. Return to the pan and heat to boiling point. Pour into beakers, top with a teaspoonful of natural yogurt and sprinkle with grated block carob.

Carob Night-Cap
(Serves 2)

¾ pint (425ml) milk
1 tablespoonful carob powder
2 teaspoonsful honey or raw cane sugar
block carob to grate

Heat the milk, carob powder, honey or sugar together in a pan. When warm, place in a blender and blend for about 20 seconds. Return to the pan, heat to boiling point, pour into beakers and sprinkle with grated block carob.

Carob Egg Nog
(Serves 2)

¾ pint (425ml) milk
2 eggs
1 tablespoonful carob powder
2 teaspoonsful honey or raw cane sugar
2 measures of dark rum or brandy

Place one egg in each beaker or heat resistant glass and whisk lightly with a fork. Heat the milk in a pan and stir in the carob powder and honey. Before the milk reaches boiling point, pour into a blender and blend at high speed for about 20 seconds. Return the milk to the pan and heat to boiling point. Pour onto the eggs, stirring continuously. Stir in the rum or brandy to taste. Serve immediately.

Carob Health Drink
(Serves 2)

¾ pint (425ml) milk
1 tablespoonful carob powder
2 teaspoonsful Brewer's yeast
2 teaspoonsful honey
block carob to grate

Put the milk in a pan to warm. Pour into a blender together with the carob powder, brewer's yeast and honey and blend at high speed for about 20 seconds. Return to the pan and heat to almost boiling point. Pour into beakers, sprinkle with grated block carob and serve immediately.

6. SWEETS

Here are such delights as Carob Hazelnut Clusters, Carob Coated Almonds, Carob Fruit and Nut Clusters, Carob *Petit Fours* – traditional, ever-popular favourites made with natural, unrefined ingredients. Think how nice it would be to offer a box of natural ingredient sweets as a gift to a friend or relative, and how about serving these delicious concoctions to your guests at a dinner party with an end-of-meal coffee and liqueur. As for the family, you will doubtless find that they can eat them faster than you can make them.

Carob Coated Almonds

6 oz (175g) block carob
6 oz (175g) whole blanched almonds

Melt the carob in a bowl over a pan of hot water. Remove from the heat and stir in the almonds, making sure that they are fully coated. Separate the nuts and lay on waxed paper to set. Serve in small fluted paper cases, placing two almonds in each paper case.

Variation:
Carob makes a delicious combination with any kind of nuts. As an alternative, try coating whole Brazil nuts, cashew nuts, pecans or any of the family favourites, following the same method.

Carob Hazelnut Clusters

6 oz (175g) block carob
6 oz (175g) whole hazelnuts

Melt the carob in a bowl over a pan of hot water. When completely melted, remove from the heat and stir in the hazelnuts, coating thoroughly. Spoon three hazelnuts in a cluster onto waxed paper and leave to set. Serve in small fluted paper cases.

Variation:
Use whole shelled peanuts or almond nibs as an alternative.

Carob Fruit and Nut Clusters

6 oz (175g) block carob
3 oz (75g) almond nibs
3 oz (75g) small seedless raisins

Melt the carob in a bowl over a pan of hot water.
Remove from the heat and stir in the almond nibs and
raisins. Spoon small amounts of the mixture onto
waxed paper and leave to set. Serve in small fluted
paper cases.

Carob Coated Stuffed Dates

6 oz (175g) block carob
1 dozen whole dates
1 dozen whole blanched almonds

Remove the stones from the dates and stuff each one
with a whole blanched almond. Press the date together
so that the almond is firmly enclosed. Melt the carob
in a bowl over a pan of hot water. Dip the stuffed
dates into the melted carob, coat thoroughly and
leave to set on waxed paper. Serve in small fluted
paper cases.

Variation:
As an alternative, use pecans, Brazil nuts or walnuts
to stuff the dates.

Carob Marzipan Squares

8 oz (225g) ground almonds
1 egg, lightly beaten
1 tablespoonful clear honey
8 oz (225g) block carob, melted over hot water
   (for coating)

Mix the ground almonds, egg and honey together.
Knead the dough with the fingers – it should be fairly
soft and pliable. Roll out to about ½ inch in thickness
and cut into squares. Place in a warm spot for a little
while to dry. When the squares have dried and can be
handled easily, coat with the melted carob. Place on
waxed paper and leave to set. Serve in small fluted
paper cases.

Carob Marzipan Diamonds

Make the marzipan as above. Roll out and cut into
diamond shapes. Place a whole almond on top of
each diamond, leave aside to dry for a little while and
coat with melted carob as above.

Carob Cherry Balls

8 oz (225g) ground almonds
1 egg, lightly beaten
1 tablespoonful clear honey
2 oz (50g) Morello or Maraschino cherries
8 oz (225g) block carob, melted over hot water
   (for coating)

Drain the cherries and pat dry with a tea towel. Mix
the ground almonds, egg and honey together to make
a soft dough. Roll the marzipan out thinly and wrap
around each cherry, forming into ball shapes with the
hands. Leave to dry for a little while and then coat
with the melted block carob. Place on waxed paper to
set and serve in small fluted paper cases.

Carob Cherry Cups

12 oz (350g) block carob
small piece wholemeal sponge cake
sherry
Morello or Maraschino cherries, halved

Melt ²/₃ of the carob in a bowl over a pan of hot water.
Place two small fluted paper cases together (one
inside the other) and put a small amount of melted
carob in the bottom. Swirl the melted carob inside the
case, making sure that the sides and bottom are fully
coated. Leave to set. If the coating seems a little thin
when dry, add some more melted carob to make sure
that the cup is properly moulded.

Break a small piece of wholemeal cake into crumbs
and soak in a little sherry. Place small amounts of the
cake and sherry mixture in the bottom of each cup.
Top with half a morello or maraschino cherry.

Melt the remaining carob over hot water and
spoon on top of the cherries, making sure that the
cups are completely sealed.

Carob Petit Fours

6 oz (175g) polyunsaturated margarine
6 oz (175g) raw cane sugar
2 eggs, beaten
6 oz (175g) wholemeal flour
2 level teaspoonsful baking powder
2 tablespoonsful natural unsweetened yogurt

For almond paste
8 oz (225g) ground almonds
1 egg, lightly beaten
1 tablespoonful clear honey

For coating and decoration
8 oz (225g) block carob
glacé cherries
blanched almonds
clear honey

Cream the margarine and sugar together until light and fluffy. Gradually add the beaten eggs. Fold in the flour, baking powder and yogurt. Spoon the mixture into a greased and lined shallow baking tin (swiss roll type) and bake for about 15 minutes at 375°F/190°C (Gas Mark 5). When the cake is cool, cut into diamond, heart, triangle, circle shapes etc. with small cutters.

To make the almond paste, mix the ground almonds, beaten egg and honey together to form a soft dough. Roll out thinly. Coat the small cake shapes with clear honey and cover with the almond paste. Melt the block carob in a bowl over hot water. When melted, coat the *petit fours* and decorate with blanched almonds or *glacé* cherries.

Carob Almond Truffles

4 oz (100g) wholemeal sponge cake
4 oz (100g) ground almonds
clear honey
sherry
carob powder

Break the wholemeal sponge cake into crumbs and mix with the ground almonds. Add sufficient honey and sherry to make a fairly stiff dough. Mould the mixture into small balls with the hands and then toss in carob powder, coating thoroughly. Serve in small fluted paper cases.

Carob Fruit and Nut Truffles

4 oz (100g) wholemeal sponge cake
4 oz (100g) finely chopped blanched almonds
4 oz (100g) finely chopped seedless raisins
clear honey
sherry
carob powder

Break the wholemeal sponge cake into crumbs and mix together with the finely chopped almonds and raisins. Add enough honey and sherry to make a stiff but pliable dough. Mould into ball shapes with the hands and then toss in carob powder, making sure that the truffles are fully coated. Serve in small fluted paper cases.

RECIPE INDEX